To LeAnne

Highgrove 2017

With my best wishes
and hope to see you too
next time!

DISCOVERING
THE MEANING
OF FLOWERS

Shane

For my Godchildren: Eamonn, Ursula, Sophie and Morgan.

With love.

CLEARVIEW

Published in the UK in 2017 by Clearview Books
22 Clarendon Gardens, London W9 1AZ
www.clearviewbooks.com

A CIP record of this book is available from the British Library.
ISBN: 978-1908337-320 276

Design: Charlotte Heal Design
Photography: Jan Baldwin
Editor: Catharine Snow
Copy Editor: Chloe Colchester
Production: Simonne Waud

Disclaimer: no insects or animals were harmed in the making
of this book, including the bee, who had already met his Maker.

Printed in Europe
Colour reproduction by JK Morris Production AB

SHANE CONNOLLY

DISCOVERING THE MEANING OF FLOWERS

/

LOVE FOUND
LOVE LOST
LOVE RESTORED

INTRODUCTION

This book celebrates the beauty of flowers. But more importantly, it celebrates the bounty of nature. When I choose flowers, I want them to look and feel like the fruits of the earth, not like products off an assembly line. And when I arrange them, I want people to be enchanted by the flowers themselves. Understanding how former generations relied upon flowers, and were even able to express emotion and communicate through them, helps us rediscover their dignity, individuality and character.

It all started about twelve years ago, when I wrote a book called *The Language of Flowers*. The experience transformed the way I see them. When I took the task on, my knowledge of the language of flowers was basic at best but, as the project progressed, I noticed something surprising. Exploring this archaic floral language was opening my eyes to the beauty of flowers and, at the same time, it was opening my mind to the stories behind those flowers. Flowers had pasts. No meaning had been randomly allocated: the unique, individual histories of each flower led to a chain of specific meanings or symbolism. It was like getting to know someone, learning their life-story and meeting their family.

I'd always had a 'botanical approach' to flower arranging, where flowers are chosen with a gardener's eye and then arranged to flatter each one's individual qualities. The alternative approach generally sees flowers as generic elements of colour, structure or form; massed together to fill the void of an empty vase. And the result relies more on quantity than individuality for impact. It's rather like cooking with off-the-shelf ingredients instead of making the most of carefully chosen seasonal food.

In the highly civilized and cosmopolitan world of today we have undoubtedly lost our ancestors' deep-rooted familiarity with nature. But the language of flowers was built on that connection. So, understandably, our twenty-first-century minds struggle to comprehend how floral symbolism could have wound its way through life, literature, and the arts to even become an object of academic study—Floriography.

Meaning had been attributed to flowers for thousands of years in Europe, Asia and the Middle East but the language of flowers was 'discovered' in Turkey, at the Ottoman Court in Constantinople. There, in 1717, the wife of the British Ambassador, Lady Mary Wortley Montagu, came across a system of coded messages used by the concubines in the Sultan's Harem. It was known as 'Selam' and was simply a decorative box filled with single flowers and other natural objects, each with individual designated symbolism, used to pass information confidentially between the concubines, under the noses of the guards and eunuchs. We don't know why Lady Mary was in the harem in the first place, but we do know that she was enchanted and immediately sent similar boxes to friends back home, presumably including written instructions to help them know what she was trying to say. A seed had been sown, and slowly it grew. In 1819 Louise Cotambert, writing under the nom de plume 'Madame Charlotte de la Tour', published the first proper dictionary of floriography, 'Le Langage des Fleurs'. Some of her meanings came from the original Turkish Salem, others were the fruits of De La Tour's painstaking research into ancient mythology and plant folklore. This was a whole new ball game. Flowers could now be used as a form of coded communication. Floriography caught on and blossomed alongside the growing passion for botany. Between 1830 and 1880, De la Tour's book inspired a host of others. Each one copied, added to, adapted and discarded previous interpretations to suit the individual author's knowledge or beliefs or to accommodate some newly discovered species of flower. The result was a confusing plethora of potential floral interpretations. But, despite this confusion, flowers were increasingly being used to express and even *awaken* emotions and feelings at a time when strict etiquette supressed open communication. By the end of the nineteenth century, an understanding of the language of flowers was as important as being correctly dressed if one wanted to make one's mark in society.

It could be said that the language of flowers, as Charlotte de la Tour knew it, died in the trenches of the Somme. The First World War removed the sentimentality and restrictions of the old order and left us with red poppies as the final floral symbol to remember the loss.

Since then, we've seen communication develop from post and telephone, via fax and mobile, to the extraordinary phenomenon of social media. This has allowed us to communicate with an exchange of images that has become so un-supressed, so completely 'out-there' and so embarrassingly permanent, that we may well be reaching the point were a different visual code becomes newly relevant as we rediscover the need for discretion.

We're still obviously searching for ways to communicate more clearly, individually and meaningfully, even today. Perhaps this book will show that there is still a lot left to learn from exploring the meaning of flowers. At its simplest floral symbolism stitches our relationship with flowers back into the seasons, nature and the garden. And that makes us think of the origin of the flowers we buy, just as we now regularly do with the food we eat.

We have always used coded communication, but I'd venture to say that the language of flowers is more expressive than the emojis, text abbreviations and acronyms that pervade communication today—maybe it's a visual code just waiting for someone to re-adapt it for Instagram, Facebook and Snapchat.

But the message I take from this is quite simple: flowers are part of life, part of the living landscape and we need to re-examine our relationship with them, use them thoughtfully and respectfully, and be aware of their fragility and the potential damage we might be causing in their production.

NO.1

LOVE FOUND

/

FOUND

discovered by chance,
or unexpectedly

LOVE FOUND

The language of flowers was purposely contrived and codified to aid and abet lovers in the pursuit of love. In this first chapter, I'm concentrating on flowers that convey the exquisite palpitations of new love: the attraction, the hesitation, the flirtation, the compliments, the faltering emotions— and just a bit of lust of course.

Spring is apparently the season when a young man's thoughts turn to fancies of love. And I'm sure a young woman's do too, as there are so many symbolic spring flowers to cater for these feelings. What I find most intriguing are the stories behind those meanings.

Take the bluebell (p. 14). Until quite recently their full name was *Endymion non-scriptus*. In greek mythology, Endymion was a handsome shepherd who caught the eye of the moon goddess, Selene. Sadly she was allowed only one nocturnal visit to earth per month but spent it gazing adoringly at him as he slept (this provided a charming, early explanation of the lunar cycle). Over time, Selene grew concerned with Endymion's commitment to her, and resolved to cast him into a state of eternal sleep, to guarantee his faithfulness. Or so the legend goes, but it brings us neatly back to bluebells and how they came to symbolize constancy and humility, in memory of Selene's enduring love and the humble shepherd Endymion's endless, virtuous sleep.

Nowadays, bluebells are called *Hyacinthoides non-scripta* as they're close cousins of hyacinths. And hyacinths also began with a mythological love affair: this time between a handsome young man called Hyacinthus and the god Apollo. Unfortunately the god of the west wind, Zeyphyrus, also appreciated the boy's various charms so a spat was inevitable. A malicious gust of wind fatally re-directed a discus and Hyacinthus was killed. Apollo, distraught, caused sweet scented flowers to grow where his lover's blood had spilt. They were called hyacinths; their upturned petals the very image of his curling locks. Hyacinths also symbolize *beauty* and *constancy* in memory of Apollo's eternal love for his handsome paramour. Either would make excellent messages from a sincere admirer with honorable intentions.

As we move into summer, we obviously think of roses, and a red rose is one of the few flowers to have survived symbolically intact since the frenzied heyday of the language of flowers. It says *I love you*, and that legacy means that this most beautiful of summer flowers traditionally makes an expensive first appearance in the depths of winter for St Valentine's Day. Roses have always been associated with the many facets of love, desire and beauty. According to legend, the jealous Roman goddess of nature, Cybele, created them in an attempt to detract from her rival - the goddess of love, Venus.

Cleopatra apparently had her pillows stuffed with fresh rose petals every evening and even carpeted a room with them in an attempt to seduce Mark Anthony with their scent. He may well have had experience of other rosy evenings, given the alleged use of roses in Roman orgies. Roses have also been linked to Brahma, Buddha, Vishnu and Confucius—always as tokens of their love and gentleness. After some hesitation, perhaps because of their association with Roman decadence, the Christian Church adopted them as a symbol of the Virgin Mary, virtually rewriting their older dedication to the great Greek goddess of love, Aphrodite, centuries before. Rosary beads evoke that dedication and are still used daily in prayer today, perpetuating the link between roses and sacred love.

Rose hybridization was thriving in the mid-nineteenth century when the language of flowers was also at its peak, and as each new variety appeared, specific meanings followed. Soon all the different facets of love had a rose or a combination of roses to describe them: ranging from the thornless rose for *love at first sight*, to that quintessential Victorian rose, the musk rose, to say *capricious beauty* or, when placed over two unopened buds, *secrecy*. In fact,

I could have written this whole book based on roses alone. But I really would encourage you to look at the alternatives to a ubiquitous red rose as a token of your love. This chapter has several exquisite options to get your message across just as beautifully.

Now you might think that autumn and winter would have no seasonal flowers with symbolic links to first love. But you'd be wrong. Chrysanthemums for example, are full of loving symbolism, with different colours meaning different romantic things.

Then, as the evenings draw in, flowers can even get quite suggestive: take the gardenias (p. 29) with their promise of a *transport to ecstasy*; or the intensely scented tuberose, offering *dangerous pleasures*; and scented white jasmine hinting at *sensuality*. This was the start of the mania for orchid collecting and some, like cattlyea, could be used to offer a compliment (of sorts) with *mature charms*. That perennial winter favourite, amaryllis, is on the same wavelength with *splendid beauty*.

All these flowers would have been greenhouse grown and considered highly novel and exotic at the time, though we can buy them so much more easily today. It certainly accounts for their rather hot and tropical meanings. There are winter garden plants too like daphne, which means *I want to please you*; eucalyptus offering *protection*, and even box hedging to reassure with *constancy and friendship*.

BLUEBELL

(Hyacinthoides Hispanica Non-Scripta Hybrid)

Bluebells express *Constancy* and *Humility* in the
language of flowers—great qualities in any relationship—
and all because of the story of a mythical Greek goddess's
eternal infatuation with a humble shepherd.

Britain's native bluebells (*Hyacinthoides Non-Scripta*)
are being threatened by the invasion of a more thuggish
Spanish variety, which is interbreeding with them, to
produce hybrids like this one—still pretty, but less
delicate, and sadly un-scented too.

So why not plant native bluebell bulbs to commemorate
a romantic union? You will help to conserve the species—
and possibly reboot your relationship at the same time.
HYACINTHS also symbolize *Constancy* and are a highly
perfumed alternative.

PURPLE LILAC

(Syringa Meyeri)

Lilacs are linked to reminiscing, and purple lilac
is specifically linked to *Memories of First Love*.
Cut or growing, they are the perfect thing for old
flames—or young lovers.

JONQUIL
(Narcissus Jonquilla)

Narcissi flowers generally symbolize egotism and vanity.
But jonquils have a more useful message in the language
of love—*I Wish You Would Return My Affection*. And
a basket of these scented, spring bulbs might well help
that happen. A ripe PEAR also symbolizes *Affection* and,
with the right note of explanation, would make a quirky
alternative, a little later in the season.

   Overleaf: JONQUILS to melt the heart with FORGET-
ME-NOTS, the symbol of *True Love*; blue and white
BLUEBELLS for *Constancy* and *Humility*; MAGNOLIA
to represent *Nobility of Heart*; PURPLE LILAC to
recall *First Love*; CORNFLOWERS for *Delicacy* and
Refinement and SWEETPEAS, to add the promise of
Delicate Pleasures ...

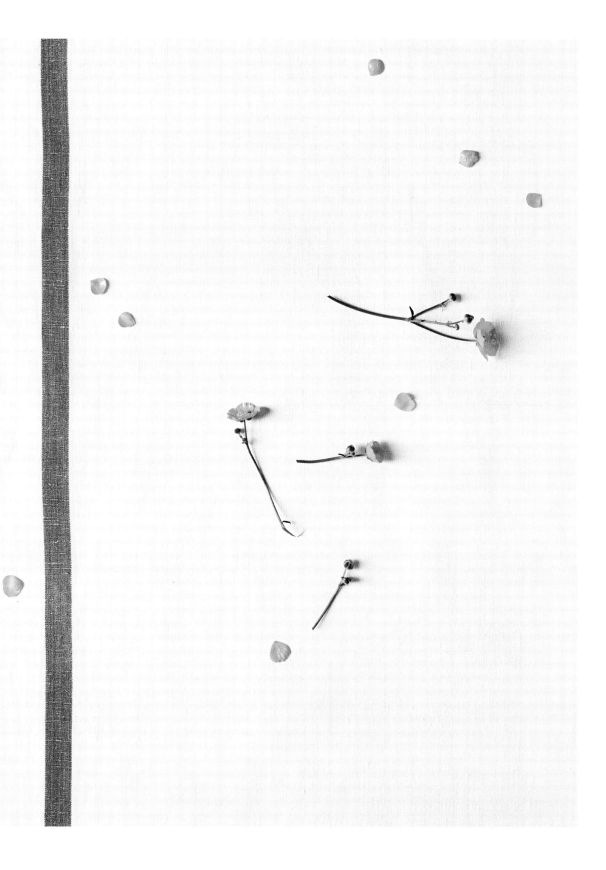

BUTTERCUPS

(Ranunculus Acris)

Buttercups are so redolent of carefree summer days that
it's hardly surprising they came to symbolize *Cheerfulness*
and *Childishness* in the language of flowers. If you prefer
not to have buttercups in your garden, MARJORAM is a
symbol of *Happiness*.

   Overleaf: I mixed buttercups with a few other flowers
to make a table-scape that is the epitome of those halcyon
days: WHITE LILAC reminds us of *Youthful Innocence*;
COW PARSLEY suggests *Fantasy*; VIOLETS are for
Innocence, Modesty and *Decency* and AURICULAS are
the symbol of *Art and Painting*.

RED ROSES

(Rosa 'Piano' and Rosa 'Darcy Bussell')

Everyone knows the meaning of a red rose. The cut-flower trade
certainly does, and, at great expense, imports several million
un-seasonal red roses for St Valentine's Day each year. All so that
lovers can say *I Love You* in the prescribed way. I hope this book
will give you some alternatives but, in the meanwhile, did you know
that there are eloquent floral replies to these rosy declarations
of love? Returning a SINGLE ROSE LEAF says, *There's Hope.*
Sending back a WITHERED ROSE is an unambiguous botanical
Slap In The Face.

The red rose is not the only rose in the language of love.

Here's a summer seduction with just a handful of garden roses, a few beech stems and three tropical gardenia flowers. The combined scent is almost as ravishing as their hidden message: BEECH for a *Lover's Tryst*; hairy little MOSS ROSES for *Voluptuousness*; a MOSS ROSE BUD for *Whispered Love*; SINGLE ROSES say *I Will Always Love You* and then the GARDENIAS with their naughty promise of a *Transport to Ecstasy*. Who needs red roses?

MAKING A VERY AMOROUS DINNER TABLE

STEP 1:

A collection of small vases gives maximum impact with
the minimum amount of flowers. I love these old glass
bottles and have collected an embarrassing amount of
them over the years. I find them ideal for a single flower
or a few small stems.

STEP 2:

Work out which flowers work best in each container:
a bottle with a larger base will help balance a heavy
headed flower and a tall thin-necked one will help hold
wispy flowers or foliage in a more upright way, to add
a bit of height.

STEP 3:

Start with the largest flowers, in this case the roses.
Having picked the ideal container for each stem, make
them sit exactly as you want, with foliage to support
them if necessary. Then tackle the smaller bits like the
rose buds and delicate gardenias.

STEP 4:

Now it's time for my favorite bit: style them singly and
in groups on a tabletop. Sometimes I work them into a
formal repeat pattern but I often find that a looser, more
chaotic approach looks better.

PINK PEONY
(Paeonia Lactiflora 'Mother's Choice')

Every year I look forward to the annual avalanche of
peonies heralding the start of summer. For centuries
they were thought to have healing powers; they got their
name from Paean, senior physician to the Greek gods.
Later they were associated with the Virgin Mary, the
'Rose Without Thorns', and became symbols of *Devotion*,
especially in marriage. And there's another link, perhaps
through Chinese literature, to *Bashfulness* and *Blushing*.
The peony season is brief and I'm always sad when it ends
but they're never quite the same when they're forced or,
even worse, held back in a cold room.

A declaration of earnest young love in a jug of flowers: PEONIES for *Modesty* and *Devotion*; a stem of PIGGYBACK PLANT symbolizes *Sweet Young Love*; a flowerless trail of SWEETPEA to promise *Pure* and *Delicate Pleasures*. And then the compliments: SMOKE BUSH symbolizing *Rare Beauty*; a trail of JASMINE for *Amiability*; three unusual white CORNFLOWERS for *Delicacy* and *Refinement*, SCENTED VIBURNUM for *Sweet and Kind*, and ANGELICA says *You Inspire Me*.

Here's the perennial favourite, the tied posy. It's
much easier to make than people think, (I show
you how on the next page) and so much nicer
when you use fragrant, seasonal, local flowers,
as I have here. The main flowers are deliciously
scented SWEETPEAS that promise *Delicate
Pleasures*. I've added PEPPERMINT for *Warmth*
and *Cordiality*; FUCHSIA the symbol of *Humble
Love*; and finally SWEET WILLIAM that offers
Gallantry and pleads, *Will You Smile?*

HOW TO TIE A LOVING BUNCH

STEP 1:

When you're making a tied bunch, good preparation
is the key. So make sure all the flowers have been
conditioned and had a good drink, then remove all
the lower foliage and line everything up neatly on
your work surface.

STEP 2:

I like tied bunches to look natural and wild so I start
with a few shapely bits of foliage held loosely in one
hand, with the stems crossing over at one point, and
then arrange them to establish the general size and
outline I want.

STEP 3:

I can now pad out this shape with fuller flowers, like
Sweet Williams. Make sure no flower is at the same
level as its neighbor for a more natural look. Thread in
the more delicate flowers, like sweet peas, last of all.

STEP 4:

At this point, the bunch is still malleable so make sure
you're completely happy before tying it off firmly with
garden string. Instead of ribbon I'm using this recycled
Indian fabric rope and I've trimmed the stems before
putting the bunch into cool water.

DANDELION

(Taraxacum Species)

One may not want dandelions in one's garden but
they are edible, drinkable, and medicinal—and they keep
children amused for hours. So they're not to be completely
dismissed. If you can catch a floating seed, you can make
a wish. So they mean, *A Wish Come True*. The snail
symbolizes patience—essential when waiting for wishes
to come true.

    Overleaf: Some wishful thinking with RANUNCULUS
to say, *I am Dazzled with Your Charms* and RED
CAMELLIAS adding *You Set My Heart on Fire.*

DAISY

(Erigeron Karvinskianus)

A daisy symbolizes *Beauty, Innocence* and *Simplicity* in the language of flowers. But I have a confession to make, this pretty thing isn't the native wild daisy they had in mind. This is a well-behaved Mexican version, and one that I love having in my garden.

Grouping vases together can make a few flowers look much more impressive—and these three hold some stary-eyed messages. DAISIES say *Beauty, Innocence* and *Simplicity*. Then there's a THORNLESS ROSE (in this case *Rosa Banksia*) symbolizing *Love at First Sight*. Add COWPARSLEY for *Fantasy* and MARJORAM for *Blushes* and *Happiness*. White CAMASSIAS say *I Can't Live Without You* (they are related to asparagus and were part of the staple diet of Native American Indians and the First Settlers). Large OX-EYE DASIES represent a *Gift or Token*, and finally a single ROSE LEAF to ask *Can I Hope?*

NO.2

LOVE LOST

/

LOST

taken away,
cannot be recovered

LOVE LOST

In Shakespeare's 'A Midsummer Night's Dream', Lysander tries to comfort his lover, Hermia, with the well-known adage that "the course of true love never did run smooth." That could certainly be the subtitle of this chapter as I look at flowers symbolising the more tortured aspects of love. You'll find that every destructive thought is catered for and every pang of heartache has its floral namesake.

Just as spring seems to be the season for love, you might expect unpleasant emotions to be communicated through poisonous weeds, or the fading blooms of autumn and winter. Certainly autumn leaves (p. 87) convey *melancholy*, and vicious brambles (pp. 66; 76) perfectly embody *difficulties*. But at first glance, few flowers deserve the negative meanings they were given in the first place. Until we look at their pasts....

Take columbines (p. 58) or aquilegias, for example. You can spot them in religious medieval paintings and tapestries as they are the ancient emblem of the dove-like Holy Spirit. But the Reformation reformed columbines too and they became the sign of a cuckold as the spurs look like the horned hat a cuckolded man was made

to wear. By the time the language of flowers came along, that was all far too embarrassing and so they were used to symbolise *capriciousness* and *folly* instead—the very qualities that probably caused a cuckold's problems in the first place!

Narcissi are another example. They symbolize *narcissism*, *vanity* and *blatant egotism* and all because of Ovid's tale of Narcissus, the beautiful youth who broke Echo's heart by his constant rejection of her love. As a punishment, the gods led Narcissus to a pool where he saw his reflection for the first time, became transfixed and remained staring at himself until he withered away. Narcissus flowers grew where his beautiful, vain body had been. The name Narcissus is also linked with the Greek word for narcotic, as the scent of narcissi was considered strong enough to overwhelm anyone.

Scent also caused a spot of bother for some particularly beautiful summer flowers. Mock orange blossom (pp. 79; 80; 84) and Mexican orange blossom (p. 80) both symbolize *counterfeit* and *fraudulence*. And that's only because their orange blossom scent impersonates another flower. In the same way Hesperis symbolizes *deceit* because it is perfumed in the evening and scentless all day (and it's name, hesperis, comes from 'Vespers' or evening prayers). The scent of lavender (p. 66) was used in laundries in the days before chemicals and deodorant, and in houses too, to help camouflage the general stench of everyday life, very much as it does today, so it also symbolizes *mistrust,* as it masks the truth.

Colour also influenced meanings: yellow roses (p. 57) and also yellow French marigolds denote *jealousy*. Whilst a whole plethora of purple flowers have parallel symbolism: purple widow geranium for *melancholy*, purple scabious, (p. 69) for *mourning*, and the purple verbena (p. 72) for *regret* and *I weep for you.*

Which leads us neatly to the rather delicate subject of flowers and death. The Victorians were big on death, so it's not surprising that the language of flowers offers many meaningful flowers to help us through that time. And of course one of them is Rosemary. It's one of the few plants whose symbolism of *remembrance* endures, and it might be more than symbolic: it's long been known that rosemary has an effect on blood circulation and ancient Greek scholars wore wreaths of rosemary to increase the blood supply to their straining brains. So it is linked to life and rejuvenation as well and I like to add it to funeral arrangements to add that positive meaning to the overall message. Of course funerary wreaths are a very ancient tradition. When Howard Carter discovered the tomb of the Egyptian boy-Pharaoh Tutankhamen, in 1922, he was deeply moved to find garlands of withered flowers within the vault and also inside the nested sarcophagi and golden coffins. So ancient Egyptians wore garlands of flowers in mourning,

and they placed them in the tombs of loved ones, much as we cast floral tributes today.

When we finally reach autumn and winter, the possibilities for miserable meanings really do come into their own. Anemones (p. 66) have Greek mythology to thank for finding themselves the symbols of *desertion* and *betrayal*. In some versions they sprang from Aphrodite's tears, in others from Adonis's blood. Either way, Adonis had died and Aphrodite felt abandoned. But she recovered all too quickly and that established their other link with *the transience of love.*

Hydrangeas first arrived from America in 1788 and their excessive demands for water during their initial trans-Atlantic voyage established their reputation as floral prima donnas. This, coupled with the fact that their flamboyant flowers seemed to change colour in unpredictable ways (which we now know is caused by the acidity of the soil) explains why they became symbols of *vanity*.

There are so many flowers with negative meanings that it's hard to imagine how they might have been used. Were they sent by rejected lovers to wreak havoc on the conscience of their unrequited, or un-ignited flames? Were they exchanged between friends to offer discreet comfort when love's course was run? Or were they used as a forewarning of danger? If that's the case, they might still have a positive role to play in our communication today.

Life is not a bed of roses. And you certainly wouldn't want it to be a bed of *YELLOW* ROSES. Their meanings in the Language of Flowers range from *Infidelity*, via *Jealousy* to the *Decline of Love*. None of this is good.

The dead bee only adds to the misery. In Indian mythology, bees symbolize the sweetness of love—and it's potential sting too.

WHITE COLUMBINE
(Aquilegia Vulgaris)

Columbine comes from the Latin *columba,* or dove, and
the flowers do look like a circle of doves. But looks can be
deceiving: they're also the ancient emblem of a *Cuckold,*
but later symbolizing *Capriciousness* and *Folly.*

  I still love them, and try to think of doves instead.

This collection has some of some of my favourite, easy-to-grow, spring garden flowers but their hidden meanings read like a salacious bit of gossip from a floral tabloid. The COLUMBINES tell of *Cuckoldry, Capriciousness* and *Folly*; dark HELLEBORES symbolize the inevitable *Lies* and *Scandal* that follow; and YELLOW PEONIES add *Shameful Blushes*. It always ends in tears. And for that we have a few ALLIUMS, a symbol of *Tears*—they are, of course, members of the onion family.

FOXGLOVE

(Digitalis Purpurea)

Foxgloves are one of the best early summer flowers to use
in tall arrangements. They last well too.

I particularly love using them as growing plants, so
that they can be planted out in the garden after the party.
But foxgloves are highly toxic. Ingested they can even be
lethal—so it's hardly surprising that they came to represent
Insincerity and *Selfish Ambition.*

There's a flower to suit every emotional crisis. This selection
shows how to get to the root of the problem. Is it FOXGLOVE—
Insincerity and *Selfish Ambition*, or BUGLOSS—*Dishonesty?*
Perhaps it's HYDRANGEA—that's *Heartlessness*, or simply
BORAGE—*Rudeness* and *Bluntness*?

   To describe how that makes you feel try LAVENDER,
for *Mistrust*; BRAMBLE for *Suffering* and *Difficulty*; or
JAPANESE ANENOME for feelings of *Desertion* and *Betrayal*.
But if one of you sells your story, you might well need TULIPS,
Fame and *Renown*.

The funeral of someone you love is always going
to be a painful experience. Flowers have been part
of rites of burial since antiquity and can bring
extraordinary comfort and consolation, particularly
when they're chosen thoughtfully. Start with old
favorites, or flowers with happy family memories.
I've chosen some with especially pertinent meanings for this arrangement.

ROSEMARY is the well-known symbol of
Remembrance. MICHAELMAS DAISY, or
September flower, is one of the last things to flower
in the summer garden and symbolizes *Farewells*.
PURPLE SCABIOUS is an emblem of *Mourning*
and finally BELL FLOWERS—campanulas—
express *Gratitude*.

MAKING A MEANINGFUL FUNERAL WREATH

STEP 1:

The technicalities of funeral wreaths are challenging:
water spills, tied bunches wilt and floral foam is pernicious because it doesn't biodegrade. So I am constantly
trying out alternatives. I am testing a new clay based
product here, which is 100% natural and may well be
the answer.

STEP 2:

Always start arrangements with the toughest stems so
that more delicate things are kept pristine and added
last. I make a rough outline with shapely bits of rosemary. The aim is to make an artistic shape. Don't worry
about spaces or gaps.

STEP 3:

Next start adding the flowers. Remember: always let
flowers be themselves—look for the most attractive
quality of each type of flower and exploit it. For example,
I use these elegant, arching stems of campanula to add
grace and movement and not to simply fill gaps.

STEP 4:

Add the other flowers, always placing the larger headed
ones at different levels to avoid a solid, chunky effect.
I fill any gaps with clusters of September flowers and
short scabious. Remember to spray regularly with cool
water until it's needed.

PURPLE VERBENA
(Verbena Bonariensis)

In the language of flowers Purple Verbena symbolizes *Regret* and says, *I Weep For You*. Not what you'd expect for such a fashionable flower. But this is one of the many times where symbolic meanings lead us into a flower's unique history, to help us appreciate them even more. In the ancient world verbenas were strongly linked with *Ritual Sacrifice, Sacred Tears* and the *Divine*. Subsequently, Christian folklore described them growing at the foot of the Cross and being used to staunch Christ's wounds. The meaning suddenly makes sense.

A broken heart is utterly desolating. But ancient meanings given
to flowers help us understand that it's always been part of human
experience. The causes don't seem to change much either.

LOVE-IN-A-MIST, or NIGELLA, says *You Confuse Me*;
You Puzzle Me; a LETTUCE is the symbol of *A Cold Heart*; CRAB
APPLES represent *Bad Temper*; RUE shows *Disdain*; a branch of
LICHEN is the symbol of *Dejection* and *Solitude*; and PURPLE
VERBENA is for endless *Regret*, and says *I Weep For You*.

A good friend will be sympathetic, but a best friend will try to stop you falling into the same old trap.

So I have a BEGONIA plant to help broach the subject, as it says *Beware*. Then the FLYTRAP represents *Deceit* and *Duplicity* (just think of the poor fly) and finally some BRAMBLES symbolize *Trouble* and *Difficulty*, as there may well be trouble ahead. I like using plants decoratively like this and the sprays of fruiting brambles in little tubes of water add an interesting, and appropriately barbed, twist.

MOCK ORANGE BLOSSOM
(Philadelphus purpurascens)

Mock Orange Blossom symbolizes *Counterfeit*
and *Fraudulence* in the language of flowers. It
breaks my heart that something I love so much has
such a terrible meaning. Of course it all happened
simply because it's 'mock' and not 'real' orange
blossom. I still plant it in my garden regardless—
and use it in arrangements when it's in season.

A simple glazed jug full of fragrant flowers is one of my favourite things.
Yet MEXICAN ORANGE BLOSSOM blossom suffers from the same
fate as mock orange blossom—because its scent is not the real deal it
also signifies *Fraudulence*. HESPERIS is another flower symbolizing
Deceit, because it only releases its perfume by night, and not by day.
MEADOW RUE is for *Disdain*. Because rues were used to induce
miscarriages—and that was definitely contemptible. LUPINS symbolize
Rejection as they were mistakenly believed to rob soil of nutrients and
so just weren't welcome. ALLIUMS are cousins to onions so *Tears*
are the obvious association and finally add MAIDEN'S TEARS for
Rejection. Perhaps the cause of the maiden's tears in the first place.

Another favourite jug filled with garden flowers (jugs really are one of the easiest containers to arrange things in!) This time the floral meanings tell someone in emotional distress to stand firm. Who said relationships were easy? The tiny vase of HEARTSEASE starts sympathetically with *I've been thinking about you.* RHUBARB, with its ancient medicinal background, symbolizes *Advice*; FENNEL is for *Strength*, and GRASSES are for *Perseverance.*

But one should never glaze over the problem either: choose from BORAGE—*Rudeness,* or MOCK ORANGE—*Fraudulence,* or even CATMINT—*Odd behavior* or *Madness.*

HOW TO TELL A STORY WITH FLOWERS:

STEP 1:

The language of flowers originated in Turkish harems.
Flowers and other items, all with secret meanings, were
put in pretty boxes and passed between concubines.
My old paper-lined tray echoes that, and starts the story
with DEAD ROSES symbolizing *Rejected Love*.

STEP 2:

New elements can alter the tone of the message
already in place. I'm channeling sentimentalism, adding
AUTUMN LEAVES for *Melancholy* (why is autumn
always gloomy?) a HANDKERCHIEF TREE FRUIT
for *Tears* (it's all in the name) and DRIED BEANS
for *Exhaustion*.

STEP 3:

Enthusiasts developed ways to extend the natural
seasons of flowers, so that coded communications
could continue all year around. Dried and pressed
flowers became hugely popular. So I added a dried
THISTLE, aptly representing *Retaliation* and a
pressed PRIMULA, pleading for *Restraint*.

STEP 4:

Finally a fresh sprig of ARTEMESIA, to suggest
Absence (it is the main ingredient of the notorious
Absinthe) and RASPBERRIES, for *Remorse*. The
language of flowers is a primitive visual system of
coded messaging—just waiting to go viral on Snapchat,
or Instagram.

A STRIPED GARDEN PINK
(Dianthus 'cherry daiquiri')

There are two ways to decline a proposal:
compassionately—with a striped carnation,
symbolizing regret that love is not mutual;
or callously—with a STRIPED GARDEN
PINK like this one, which is a blunt *Refusal.*

LOVE RESTORED

/

RESTORED

to re-establish,
return to original condition

LOVE RESTORED

Buddha is often quoted as having said, "Health is the greatest gift, contentment the greatest wealth, faithfulness the best relationship". And those wise words sum up the sentiments in this last chapter to perfection. Here, I look at flowers with specific links to a loving, contented life. These are the flowers to choose when you've found love, gone through its initial trials and tribulations, and have finally decided to settle down to secure, domestic bliss.

Sometimes this may even lead to a wedding–naturally every flower designer's favourite word! Flowers play a huge part in the look and feeling of the 'Big Day'. Even a few references to the language of flowers can make the flowers you choose much more meaningful.

I am particularly fond of using flowers with reassuring, hopeful meanings in wedding bouquets. In spring we're spoilt for choice, with snowdrops kicking it all off as soon as the earth unfreezes. They were a sign of *hope* for our ancestors and continue to be so today. Queen Victoria chose them for her wedding bouquet in February 1840, when the future of the monarchy depended upon her Marriage, and the heirs it might bring.

Hawthorn flowers only when the weather is getting warmer and it was also a sign of hope long before the language of flowers made it official. In England it's known as Mayflower, after the month in which it usually flowers. And that's the name the Pilgrim Fathers gave their ship as they set sail for the New World, undoubtedly with that in mind.

Another great May-time flower is lily of the valley (pp. 96, 98), and it is one of my favourite flowers of the whole year. If heaven exists, I'm sure it is perfumed with lily of the valley. Again, it's a cautious flower and blooms only when the weather gets warmer and there's no danger of its flowers being damaged by frost. For centuries farmers have used it as a natural barometer, its flowers in effect heralding the arrival of summer. Appropriately then, it symbolizes *the return of happiness*. It is also listed with the alternative meaning *you have made my life complete* in some floral lexicons, but either meaning makes it the symbolic floral *sine qua non* to include in any spring wedding bouquet.

Summer roses obviously appear in this chapter as well. They have been associated with physical as well as emotional wellbeing for several hundred years. In Arabia they were the basis of a cure for tuberculosis and in Britain, the sixteenth century herbalist Gerard recommended a distillation of roses to 'strengthen the heart, refresh the spirits and help you sleep'. Rosehip syrup was still given to babies as a source of vitamin C well into the twentieth century, and rose water continues to refresh many beautiful complexions around the world today. So roses are particularly bound up with a life of health, happiness and contentment. Appropriately then, pink roses (pp. 95, 104) represent *perfect happiness*; whilst white roses (pp. 121, 122) are another popular wedding flower saying *I am worthy of you*.

White lilies symbolize *purity* and are a traditional companion to white roses at weddings. They now come in a bewildering range of types and colours and that has, thankfully, removed most of their superstitious association with death. There is some truth in the tale though as the strong scent of lilies was 'useful' around corpses in the past. I particularly like the symbolism behind Turk's cap lilies (p. 126) as they promise *with my whole heart*—most probably derived from their use in both tribal medicine and herbalism to relieve heart disease and cardiac pain.

Several clinging and climbing plants have relevant meanings for this chapter, their physical abilities clearly excellent horticultural metaphors for a close and binding relationship: honeysuckle (p. 119) has long been associated with *contented love* and *marital fidelity* and in folklore it's thought to bring good luck and protection to any house it grows on; also there is jasmine (p. 108), which reminds us to be *good natured* and *amiable* with our other-half.

But there's also wisteria, which symbolizes mutual trust and, rather more literally, *I cling to you,* and passionflower to symbolize *fervent devotion*. Finally there is bindweed – that most pernicious of clingers, to say *let us unite*. Knowing the plant, the union or attachment it has in mind is going to be quite permanent.

At the beginning of autumn, we can find the beautiful spindle berry and its endearing romantic message *your image is engraved on my heart*.

This reminds me of a story behind the aromatic evergreen, bay (p. 126). In ancient Greek legend, Apollo was again on the rampage. This time he was in hot pursuit of a beautiful nymph called Daphne. As she ran, she called out to the gods for help and they responded to her request by turning her into a bay tree. Perhaps not quite what she had in mind, but Apollo, distraught, wove himself a wreath of bay to remember her by. And because of poor Daphne, a bay leaf has the message *forever true* in the language of flowers.

Tough, evergreen plants often have associations with endurance and stoicism in relationships, so fit well into this chapter. Myrtle has symbolized love and *a contented married life* since ancient times. Ivy is another perfect example: a single leaf (p. 116) symbolizes friendship but the continuous strand of ivy leaves (pp. 98, 120) symbolizes a *happy marriage* and reminds us that an attachment based on enduring friendship is at the core of any contented relationship.

PINK ROSES

(Rosa 'Sharifa Asma' and Rosa 'Constance Spry')

If a red rose reflects the fires of passionate love,
perhaps a pink one can convey the gentle glow on a
healthy, contented cheek. I'm sure that's why they became
the symbol of *Perfect Happiness*. So pink roses, of any
shade, are an apt choice for a summer wedding. I once
used tall, growing pink rose-trees, and the newly-weds
took them back and planted them at home afterwards.
Now they celebrate every anniversary in their rose
garden—perfectly 'happy ever after'.

LILY-OF-THE-VALLEY
(Convalleria Majalis)

Lily-of-the-valley will never flower before all danger
of frost has passed. They're the ancient harbinger
of warmer weather and that's one reason why they
symbolize *The Return Of Happiness.*

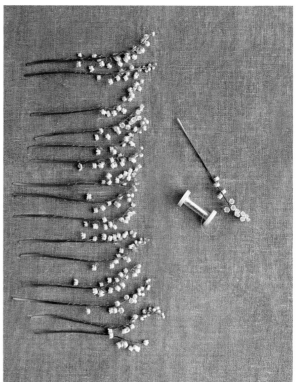

MAKING A CROWN OF HAPPINESS

STEP 1:

An intricately wired floral headdress is not something
to attempt for the first time on your wedding day!
You'll need a selection of floristry wires, floral tape,
some ribbon, a length of millinery wire (to fit around
your head) and well-conditioned flowers.

STEP 2:

Wiring lily-of-the-valley is an old-fashioned florist's skill,
which helps stop the delicate stems drooping too quickly.
The finest wire is delicately spiraled along each stem
and between every bell. Re-cut the finished stem and put it
into water whilst you wire more.

STEP 3:

Ivy leaves are wired with a tiny 'stitch' through the
central vein, a supporting loop, with the ends twisted
along the stem. Lily of the valley is clustered, 'sealed'
with floral tape and bound firmly onto the millinery
wire, alternating with ivy leaves.

STEP 4:

Keep binding until your length of millinery wire is
completely covered with flowers and ivy. A loop at each
end will be necessary to attach the ribbon, as tying the
finished flower crown onto the head is the best way to
get an accurate fit.

IRIS

(Iris 'Benton Dierdre')

Iris, the Greek messenger goddess, was thought to slide
regularly down to earth on a rainbow. So it fits that these
multi-colored namesakes bring a message of *Good News*.

GLORY LILY
(Gloriosa Rothschildiana Lutea)

Officially these exotic beauties symbolize *The Sublime
Union of The Lover and His Beloved.* In modern
parlance I think one might safely say they mean that
Love Has Been Fully Restored. Choose these sexy
flowers to celebrate any romantic union or reunion.
You can buy them both as cut flowers or growing plants.

ARRANGING A BOWL OF CONTENTMENT

STEP 1:

Arranging flowers in a bowl can be a real challenge.
Chicken wire and flower pins can help. Others use floral
foam (which I'd rather avoid). An alternative is to put
a few small containers or jam-jars into the bowl.

STEP 2:

You can now arrange flowers into, and between the
containers. This makes the basis of a framework
to anchor the heavier stems and help long shapely
pieces stand upright too. I always start with shape
and flow in mind, and never worry about gaps or
spaces at this stage.

STEP 3:

Some of the larger flowers, like Solomon's Seal, can
now be threaded through the supportive grid of stems
already in the containers and they will stay perfectly
in place. Group things like this together, in one area,
to give that 'garden-gathered' effect.

STEP 4:

Finally the most delicate flowers—in this case the fully
open garden roses—can be added to the arrangement.
This way you avoid bruising them with other stems. They
fill most gaps beautifully and short pieces of foliage soon
sort out the rest.

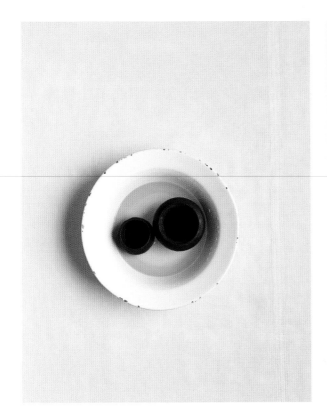

This arrangement could be called 'The Secret of Contentment'. With these flowers, you can be assured that all your symbolic foundations for a happy relationship are covered.

HONESTY, really does symbolize *Honesty* and *Sincerity*; JASMINE reminds us to be *Good Natured* and *Amiable*; PINK CRANESBILL is for *Generosity* (but be careful, its blue brother is for envy); then there's HAWTHORN to symbolize *Hope*, without which all is lost. Finally SOLOMON'S SEAL to bring *Permanence* and sets *The Seal of Love Over All*—and the result—PINK ROSES and *Perfect Happiness*!

PASSIONFLOWER
(Passiflora Caerulea)

Passionflowers have had a checkered past. Ancient
Aztec Priests and Kings cultivated the 'Snake Vine'
and used its extract as a narcotic to sedate humans
prior to sacrifice. Then the Spanish Conquistadores
came along and re-interpreted them as a holy symbol
of Christ's passion. The Pope declared them miraculous
and soon Passionflowers were being painted and carved
on Christian altars to symbolize the equally zealous
convictions of a different age. The language of flowers
diluted this to *Fervent Devotion*—in a romantic sense.

WILD STRAWBERRY

(Fragaria Vesca)

The Romans thought wild strawberries were the fruits of
Elysium. The language of flowers rightly decided they'd be
the symbol of *Perfect Goodness*. I'd encourage everyone
to grow them and taste one. And then you'll see why.

MAKING A MEANINGFUL BUTTONHOLE

STEP 1:

The groom tends to draw the floral 'short straw' at
weddings, so it's fun to make meaningful and unusual
buttonholes for a change. Each element is wired using
fine wire and floral tape—it's one of the best ways to
learn wiring techniques.

STEP 2:

Always wire the toughest ingredients first: so start with
some ivy leaves in the way shown on page 99. The rose
leaves are done in a similar way but the strawberries
need only a simple loop and a twist down each stem.

STEP 3:

Now group the ingredients together between your fingers
and tweak them until all the leaves are facing the right
way and everything looks balanced. Avoid making them
too large and heavy. A simple twist of wire and floral tape
holds everything securely.

STEP 4:

Traditional suits have a buttonhole in the lapel to hide
this wired stem. But it's also fashionable to decorate it
and leave it on show. Here I've wrapped it in wired string,
which you can buy from most florists. Don't forget to
add a pin or two.

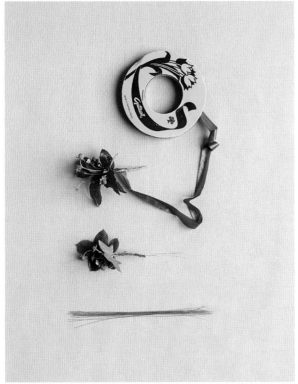

These buttonholes are full of meanings and are just the thing to make a groom feel special on his big day.

We already know that WILD STRAWBERRIES describe *Perfect Goodness*, and an IVY LEAF is the symbol of *Friendship* and two or three together symbolize a *Happy Marriage*. Then from the first chapter you might remember ROSE LEAVES and how they say *You Can Hope* if sent as a reply to an admirer's gift of roses. Here they sum it all up and say *My Hopes Have Been Rewarded*.

COMMON HONEYSUCKLE

(Lonicera Peliclymenum)

Unlike the passionflower, the honeysuckle has had an unblemished past and has always been happily associated with good things: *Devoted Love*, *Fidelity* and *Loyalty*. It's even appeared in stylized forms in jewelry, iron work, paintings, carvings and architecture over the centuries as a recurring symbol of the contented home. It represents the best qualities of constancy and devotion, especially in matrimony. Perhaps that's because its sweet scented flowers cling gently, without harming—like ideal love.

This bowl is completely overflowing with auspicious wedding symbolism. Joining our old friends HONEYSUCKLE, IVY and WILD STRAWBERRIES, respectively signifying the essentials of *Devoted Love* and *Fidelity, A Happy Marriage,* and *Perfect Goodness*; are two flowers which voice every couples' hopes on their wedding day: WHITE PHLOX evokes *The Perfect Union of Hearts and Souls* and WHITE ROSES which are happy to say *I Am Worthy Of You.* They are a perfect combination for a summer wedding bouquet or table decoration.

FERN

(Polystichum)

Victorians were passionate about ferns. In fact, between 1840 and 1900, their interest in them developed into an obsession, and an international craze. So it's not surprising they came to represent *Fascination* in the floral dictionaries being compiled at that time.

Overleaf, ferns are the basis of another simple and meaningful wedding day arrangement with LIME BRANCHES, the ancient emblem of *Marriage* and *Wedded Love*; TURK'S CAP LILIES adding *With My Whole Heart*; BAY with its promise to be *True Forever*; and SAGE making sure it *will* be forever with its promise of a *Long and Healthy Life*.

DAHLIA
(Dahlia 'Café au Lait')

Dahlias are currently enjoying a bit of well-deserved
revival in the world of floral haute couture. None more
so than this sophisticated little number called Café au
Lait. But, along with carnations and chrysanthemums,
dahlias have been on a bit of a fashion rollercoaster.
So its only very recently that their symbolic association
with *Good Taste* and *Elegance* has started to seem fitting
again. *Good Taste* may have come from 'good to eat'
because dahlia tubers were originally imported as a
potato substitute.

CURRANTS convey a lovely message in the language of flowers: *You Please Everyone.* Probably because they traditionally had great medicinal value and were especially used to treat infections. Combined here with DAHLIAS, for *Taste* and *Elegance,* they certainly do please the eye. I love using fruit decoratively and though dahlias and currants might have *first* met on a vegetable patch, I've put them in these posh glass vessels and enjoy this juxtaposition enormously for a romantic dinner table.

GLOSSARY

A

Acacia Concealed *Love; friendship*

Acanthus Fine *art; artifice*

Achillea (yarrow) *War; cure for heartache*

Acontie (wolfbane) *Treachery; misanthropy*

Agapanthus *Love letters*

Allium *Tears 60,63,80,82*

Almond Blossom *Hope*

Almond tree *Thoughtlessness; indiscretion*

Aloe *Grief; Bitterness; Religious Superstition*

Alstroemeria *Devotion; Friendship*

Althea (marsh mallow) *Consumed by love*

Amaranth *Fidelity Immortality unfading love*

Amaryllis Belladonna *Timidity; Beautiful but timid*

Amaryllis Hippeastrum *Splendid Beauty*

Anemone (wild) *Anticipation; Expectation*

Anemone (garden) *Pain of parting*

Anemone (japanese) *Desertion; betrayal; transience of love 66*

Angelica *You inspire me 35, 36*

Apple *Temptation;*

Apple Blossom *Repentance; Preference Good fortune*

Arbor Vitae *Unchanging Friendship*

Arbutus *Esteemed love; 'Thee only do I love'*

Artemisia *Absence 86*

Ash (mountain) *Prudence*

Ash Tree *Grandeur*

Aspen Tree *Lamentation*

Auricula *Art and Painting 24*

Autumn leaves *Melancholy 86*

Azalea *Romance; Temperance; Womanhood*

B

Bachelors Button *Hope (in love); celibacy*

Balm *Sympathy*

Balm of Gilead *Healing; cure*

Barberry *Sharpness; sour temper*

Basil *Hatred; Best wishes; Good luck*

Bay leaf *True forever 126*

Bay wreath *The reward of merit*

Bee Ophrys *Error*

Beech *Lovers' Tryst; prosperity 29, 30*

Begonia *Beware: 77*

Bell Flower *Constancy; gratitude: 69,71*

Bell Flower (small white) *Gratitude*

Belladonna *Silence*

Bells of Ireland *Good luck*

Betony (stachys officiaualis) *Surprise*

Bindweed *Let us unite*

Birch Tree *Gracefulness; meekness*

Bird of Paradise *Magnificence*

Blackthorn (sloe) *Difficulties*

Bladdernut tree *Frivolous amusement*

Bluebell *Constancy; humility; kindness 15, 20*

Borage *Bluntness; rudeness 66, 84*

Bramble *Suffering; Trouble and Difficulty 66,77*

Broom *Humility; neatness*

Bugloss *Dishonesty 66*

Buttercups *Childishness; cheerfulness 22-24*

Butterfly orchid *Gaiety*

Butterfly weed *Let me go*

C

Cabbage *Profit*

Cactus *Warmth; endurance*

Calendula *Joy*

Calla Lilly *Feminine beauty; delicacy; modesty*

Camellia (pink) *Longing for you; admiration*

Camellia (red) *You set my heart on fire 46*

Camellia (white) Perfect loveliness; you are adorable

Camassias *I can't live without you 48,50*

Camomile *Patience; energy in adversity*

Candytuft *Indifference*

Canterbury Bell *Gratitude; acknowledgement*

Carnation *Pride and beauty; Health and energy*

Carnation (clove red) *Yes!*

Carnation (deep red) *Passion; Heartbreak*

Carnation (pink) *I'll never forget you*

Carnation (purple) *Changeable; whimsical*

Carnation (striped) *A blunt Refusal*

Carnation (white) *Woman's good luck gift*

Carnation (yellow) *Disdain; You have disappointed me!*

Catalpa flower *Beware of the coquette*

Catmint *Odd behaviour; madness 84*

Cedar leaf *I live for you*

Cedar of Lebanon *Incorruptible*

Celandine *Future joys; joys to come*

Cherry Blossom *Spiritual beauty*

Chervil *Sincerity; good education*

Chestnut *Do me justice*

Chrysanthemum (chinese) *you are a great friend*

Chrysanthemum (red) *I love*

Chrysanthemum (white) *Truth*

Chrysanthemum (yellow) *Slighted love*

Chrysanthemum(rose) *In love*

Cinquefoil *Beloved child*

Clematis *Sacrifice; mental poverty; vacuous*

Clematis (evergreen) *Poverty*

Clover (four leaf) *Be mine*

Clover (white) *Think of me*

Cobaea Scandens *Gossip*

Colchicum Autumnalis *My best days are over/past*

Columbine *Cuckold; capriciousness; folly 58, 60, 62*

Convolvulus (blue) *Repose; night*

Coreopsis *Always cheerful*

Corn *Riches*

Cornflower *Delicacy; refinement 20,36*

Cockscomb *Frippery; affectation*

Cowparsley *Fantasy 24,48,50*

Cowslip *Candour; pensiveness; winning grace*

Crab apple *Bad tempered 74*

Cranberry *Cure for heartache*

Cranesbill (blue) *Envy*

Cranesbill (pink) *Generosity 104, 107,108*

Cress *Stability power*

Crocus *Cheerfulness; youthful joy*

Crown Imperial *Majesty; Power*

Cucumber *Criticism*

Currants (branch of) *You please everyone 130, 132*

Currants (flower) *Your frown will kill me*

Cyclamen *Diffidence*

Cypress *Mourning; death*

Cypress with marigold *Despair*

D

Daffodil *Regards; unrequited love; chivalry*

Dahlia *Good taste; elegance; dignity 129,130,132*

Daisy *Innocence and beauty; simplicity 47,48,50*

Daisy (ox-eye) *A gift or token 48,50*

Daisy (wild) *I will think of it*

Daisy Michaelmas *Farewell 69,71*

Damson tree (wild plum) *Independence*

Dandelion *A wish come true 42,44*

Daphne Mezereon *I want to please you*

Daphne Odora *I would not change you*

Datura *Deceitful charms*

Delphinium *Airy*

Dock *Patience*

Dogsbane *Deceit*

Dogwood (flowering cornus) *Am I indifferent to you*

Double Daisy *Participation*

Dragon Plant (dranuuculus) *A snare*

Dried Beans *Exhaustion 86*

E

Eidelweiss *Noble courage; daring*

Elder *Compassion; zealousness*

Elm *Dignity and grace*

Eucalyptus *Protection*

Eucharis Maidenly *Charms*

Evening Primrose *Inconstancy*

Evergreens *Poverty*

Everlasting Pea *Do not go away; lasting pleasures*

F

Fennel *Strength; Force 84*

Fern *Fascination; sincerity 124, 126*

Feverfew *Protection*

Field *Maple Humility*

Fig *Longevity*

Fig tree *Prolific*

Fir (tree) *Time*

Flax *I feel your kindness*

Flower-of-an-hour *Delicate beauty*

Flowering Reed *Confidence in heaven*

Flytrap *Deceipt; duplicity : 77*

Forget-me-not *True love; unforgotten : 20*

Forsythia *Expectation; anticipation*

Foxglove *Insincerity: Selfish ambition 65,66*

French Marigold *Jealousy*

Fritillary Imperialis *Majesty; power; pride of birth*

Fritillary snakeshead *Persecution*

Frog Ophrys *Disgust*

Fuchsia *Humble love 39,40*

Fumitory *Hatred*

G

Garden Marigold *Grief; chagrin; unease; comfort*

Gardenia *Transport to ecstasy 29, 30*

Garlic *Courage; strength*

Gentian *Intrinsic worth; integrity*

Geranium (ivy) *Can I have the next dance*

Geranium (lemon; nutmeg) *Unexpected meeting*

Geranium (rose) *You're my choice*

Geranium (scarlet) *Silliness; comfort*

Geranium (widow) *Melancholy*

Gernanium (oak leaf) *True friendship*

Gladiola *Love at first sight; ready armed*

Glory Lily *Sublime union; love fully restored 102*

Gloxinia *Love at first sight*

Goats' rue *Reason*

Golden Rod *Encouragement*

Gooseberry *Anticipation*

Grape vine *Drunkenness*

Grasses *Perseverance 84*

H

Handkerchief *Tree Tears 86*

Harebell *Grief; Retirement*

Hawthorn *Hope 104, 107, 108*

Hazel *Reconciliation*

Heartsease *I'm thinking of you 84*

Heather *Good Luck*

Helenium *Tears*

Heliotrope *I adore you; devotion*

Helleborus (orientalis) *Lies and scandal 60, 62*

Helleborus (niger) *Reassurance*

Hemp *Fate*

Hesperis *Deceit 80, 82*

Hibiscus *Delicate beauty*

Hippeastrum *Splendid beauty*

Holly *Foresight; domestic happiness; defence;*

Hollyhock *Fecundity; fruitfulness*

Honesty *Honesty; sincerity 104,107,108*

Honeysuckle (wild) *Devoted love; fidelity; A contented home 118,120,122*

Hop *Injustice*

Hornbeam *Resilience; Strength*

Hyacinth *Constancy 15*

Hydrangea *Heartlessness, Vanity 66*

I

Indian pink *Always lovely*

Iris *I have a message for you; Good news 101*

Iris (german) *Flame*

Ivy (leaf) *Friendship 116*

Ivy (trail) *Constancy; A happy marriage; fidelity 98,116,120,122*

J

Jasmine (J officinale) *Amiability; friendliness 34,36*

Jasmine (J polyanthum) *Sensuality*

Jonquil *I wish you'd return my affection 19,20*

Judas Three *Betrayal; betrayed*

Juniper *Protection; Succour*

K

Kingcup *I want to be rich*

L

Laburnum *Dangerous Beauty*

Larch *Boldness*

Larkspur *Fickleness; levity; hilarity*

Laurel *Wreath Glory*

Lauristinus *Don't neglect me*

Lavatera *Sweet disposition*

Lavender *Mistrust 66*

Lemon *Zest*

Lemon blossom *Discretion; fidelity in love*

Lettuce *A cold heart 74*

Polyanthus *Confidence*

Pomegranate *Foolishness; conceit; pride*

Poppy *Consolation; Oblivion to sorrow*

Poppy (red) *Remembrance*

Poppy (white) *Sleep*

Primrose *Early youth; young love; Modesty*

Primula *Restraint, Diffidence 86*

Privet *Inhibited*

Pulmouaria (lugwort) *You are my life*

Pumpkin *Greedy*

Q

Quince *Temptation*

R

Ranunculus *I am dazzled with your charms 44*

Raspberry *Remorse 86*

Reeds *Music*

Rhodedendron *Agitation; danger; beware*

Rhubarb *Advice 84*

Rose *Love; beauty*

Rose (austrian) *You are all that is lovely*

Rose (blood red) *I love you 26*

Rose (briar) *I wound to heal*

Rose (burgundy) *Unconscious beauty*

Rose (cabbage) *Love's ambassador*

Rose (china) *Beauty always new*

Rose (cinnamon) *Without pretension*

Rose (damask) *Freshness; brilliant complexion*

Rose (deep red) *Shame; bashfulness*

Rose (dog) *Pleasure and pain*

Rose (eglantine) *I wound to heal; poetry*

Rose (full blown placed over two buds) *Secrecy*

Rose (fullblown) *You are beautiful*

Rose (maiden's blush) *If you love me; you will find it out*

Rose (moss bud) *Whispered love 29,30*

Rose (moss) *Voluptuousness 29, 30,*

Rose (multiflora) *Grace*

Rose (musk) *Capricious beauty*

Rose (pink) *Perfect happiness 95, 105,107,108*

Rose (pink bud) *New Love*

Rose (pompon) *Gentility*

Rose (red and white together) *Unity*

Rose (red bud) *You are young, pure and lovely*

Rose (rugosa - Japanese rose) *Beauty is your only attraction*

Rose (single) *Simplicity; I will always love you 29, 30*

Rose (striped) *Variety is the spice of life*

Rose (tea) *I'll always remember*

Rose (thornless) *Love at first sight 48,50*

Rose (white bud) *Innocent of love; naive*

Rose (white open) *I am worthy of you 120, 122, 123*

Rose (yellow) *Infidelity; jealousy; decrease of love 57*

Rose (york and lancaster) *War*

Rose bouquet of fullblown *Gratitude*

Rose leaf *There's hope 27,48,50,115,116*

Rose withered *Rejected love 27, 86*

Rosemary *Remembrance; Commitment; fidelity 69,71*

Rue *Disdain 74*

Rye Grass *Changeable disposition*

S

Sage *A long and healthy life 126*

Salvia (blue) *I think of you*

Scabious *Unfortunate love; widowhood*

Scabious (purple) *Mourning 69,71*

Scots thistle *Retaliation*

Sedum Spectabile (ice plant) *Your look freezes me*

Shamrock *lightheartedness*

Silverleaf *Naivety*

Smilax *Delicate lovliness*

Smoke bush *Rare Beauty 34,36*

Snap dragon *Presumption; No, never!*

Snowdrop *Consolation and Hope*

Solomons Seal *Permanence; healing; Seal of love 105,107,108*

Spearmint *Warmth inside*

Speedwell *Female fidelity*

Spindletree *Your image is engraved on my heart*

Spotted Arum *Ardour; great warmth*

St John's Wort *Superstition; animosity*

Star of Bethlehem *Reconciliation; purity*

Statice *Lasting beauty*

Stephanotis *Happy marriage; come to me*

Stock *Contented life; lasting beauty;*

Stonecrop *Tranquillity*

Strawberry (wild) *Perfect goodness; excellence*
   113, 115, 116

Sunflower *Pride; haughtiness*

Sunflower (dwarf) *Your devout admirer; adoration*

Sweet pea *Delicate pleasures, 20,39,40*

Sweet Pea (without flowers) *Pure and delicate*
   pleasures 34,36

Sweet William Gallantry; *Will you smile? 39,40*

T

Thistle *Retaliation 86*

Thorn Apple *Deceitful charms*

Thyme *Strength and courage*

Trillium grandiflorum *Enthusiasm*

Trillium Pictum *Modest beauty*

Tuberose *Dangerous pleasure*

Tulip (general) *Fame; renown 67*

Tulip (red) *Declaration of love*

Tulip (striped) *You have beautiful eyes*

Tulip (yellow) *Hopeless love*

V

Verbena (purple) *Regret; I weep for you 72,74*

Verbena (white) *Pray for me*

Veronica *Fidelity*

Vetch *I cling to you*

Viburnum opulus *Heavenly Thoughts*

Viburnum (scented) *Sweet and kind.*

Viola (blue) *I'll always be true and loyal*

Viola (purple) *You are in my thoughts*

Viola (white) *Innocence; modesty; purity*

Viola (yellow) *Rural happiness*

Violet (sweet) *Innocence; modesty; decency 24*

W

Wallflower *Fidelity in adversity*

Water lily *Great beauty with coldness of heart*

Weeping willow *Melancholy*

Wheat *Wealth and prosperity*

Willow herb *Pretension*

Winter cherry *Deception*

Wisteria *I cling to you; mutual trust 93*

Witch hazel *A spell is on me*

Woodbine *Sweet disposition*

Woodruff *Sweet humility*

Wormwood (Artemesia) *Absence*

Y

Yew (taxus) *Sorrow; penitence*

Z

Zinnia (mixed) *Thoughts of absent friends; I miss you*

Zinnia (scarlet) *Constancy*

Zinnia (white) *Goodness*

Zinnia (yellow) *Daily remembrance*

INDEX

A Bouquet of full blown
roses symbolizes Gratitude

Writing a book is always a huge team effort and the incomparable Jan Baldwin and Charlotte Heal deserve equal credit for the result, as well as my enjoyment of the process. The biggest bunch of bellflowers to you both. And to Catharine Snow, who helped nurture the project, both editorially, and with her delicious lunches, and commissioned it in the first place. Thanks also to Chloe Colchester for her initial edits of the text, Simonne Waud on team Clearview and Peter Dixon and Shivy Kanagaratnam on team Jan B.

My wonderful colleagues at Shane Connolly and Co had to put up with, help, and support me, throughout the process: I am deeply indebted to Beckie Stockley, Jilly Douglas and Mark Campbell; and also to the talented freelance flower artists who help us keep the show on the road: Graham Murtough, Moira Seedhouse, Jo Hughes, Paul Barratt, Nicola Scarpellini, Lily Fitch, Juan Tapia, Yollanda Chiaramello, Pel Mercer, Nataliya Andrienko, Alex Whitmore, Jeremy Martin, Byoungsung Son and Clare McKnight. My thanks also to the lifetime honorary members of the team: Tracey Gorton, Sharon Melehi, Louise Avery and Mark Lovegrove. And the essential backstage crew: Paul Williams (and all at Pollencrew) and Stephen and Alison Smallwood (and all at Thorne Widgery).

What would a flower book be without the flowers? Deepest gratitude to my esteemed and talented Great British Growers: Bridget Elworthy at the Landgardeners, Polly Nicholson at

Bayntun, John and Claire Waddington at Argo Flowers Ltd. and Jane MacFarlane-Duckworth at the Flower Union.

We in London are also fortunate to have one of the best flower markets in the world and I value my friends there more than words, or flowers, can say: Dennis, Eddy and Sonny at Dennis Edwards Flowers; Saul, Mick and Bob at Pratley Covent Garden Ltd; David Gorton, Zach and Adil at GB Foliage; Richie and Bobby at Alagar Ltd; Paul at Evergreen; Dean and Craig at Quality Plants; And everyone at Zest, Bloomfield, Arnott and Mason, L. Mills, Porter's, C. Best, Donovan's, Whittington's, and The Flower Store. And of course Tony and Camilla at The Café. If we don't support our local growers and flower markets, wherever we live, there will be no language of flowers!

I would also like to express my deep gratitude to the following inspiring people for their instrumental and pivotal support and for shaping my life and career in flowers: my parents, Gerry and Peggy Connolly; Michael Goulding, Elizabeth Baker, Nigel Lake, Pulbrook and Gould, Caroline Evans-Fiennes, Margaret and Mervyn Boyd, Regina Rickless, Sylvia Took, Simon Brown, TRH The Prince of Wales and The Duchess of Cornwall and HRH The Duchess of Cambridge.

And finally, my deepest gratitude of all goes to my family, and in particular to my darling wife Candida, who really does keep my life full of pink roses—thank you.